Merrythoughts

Kay Foley

&

This book is dedicated
with love to
Cole, Peter, and Oliver.

&

Acknowledgements

ౘ

I would like to thank my family: my parents, who encouraged every creative endeavor we kids ever tried; my six siblings, especially Mary and Eileen, who collaborated with or encouraged me throughout my creative life; and my three sons, Cole, Peter and Oliver, whose artistic advice I am constantly seeking and without whom my life would be decidedly empty. Thanks to my many loving friends who make me laugh as well as offer a soft place to land when I need one; all of the fascinating artists I've met on the road; and all of the customers who've asked me to put together a book, particularly the woman who said, "You thought all this up? What an interesting brain you must have! You can't imagine how DULL life is for the rest of us."

I especially thank my good friends, Pam McClure, for her excellent critique, and Hank Botts, who supported me so much in getting this book finished at last.

Table of Contents

Foreword	i
To Dream Is To Believe	1
Life With Dogs & Other Living Creatures	14
Imagination Is Excellent	27
Love, Romance & All	40
The World of Work	55
Pondering the Bigger Questions of Life	70
Magic, the Moon & the Insanely Beautiful World in Which We Live	82
Art, Writing & Marc Chagall	95
Living Life Rightly	109

Foreword
(or What I Was Thinking)

When I was a little girl of eight or nine I wrote a set of stories about a rabbit named Twitchy, and my father sent the stories to a publisher. Although the publisher was very kind, the stories were never printed.

A dreamy girl, loving of books, stories, movies, and make-believe, I continued to write as I grew up. I wrote plays that my sisters, friends and I put on for our families, with the director's copy and separate parts for all the actors written out longhand in pencil. (I was always the director, too, of course.) I kept diaries and notebooks throughout the desert of teenage years and beyond. I bought blank books and turned them into handwritten, primitively illustrated books for my friends, sisters, sons, and lovers.

Always always the wish that I might someday publish a

real book lived and grew inside me. Year after year I wrote WRITE A BOOK at the top of my list of New Year's Resolutions.

Now I go from art show to art show and people come into my booth (you, too, possibly) and stand and read and read, and many have turned to me and said, "You should write a book!" For a long time I have said back to them, "I have always wanted to write a book." And then I was able to say, "I'm working on a book." And then, "I'm working on a book and it will be finished by fall." But I'd get very busy with shows and whatnot and I'd say, "I'm working on a book and it will be finished by spring," etc., and you get the general idea.

So you see, this book has been a LONG time in the making, oh years and years. But here it is! A work of love.

Merrythought is the old British word for what we nowadays call the wishbone of a chicken or turkey. I grew up breaking wishbones with the hope that I would end up with the long end and therefore get my wish. The older custom had it that the person with the long piece would marry first, resulting in "merry thoughts" among the participants. Since this book is so much about wishes and dreams, I felt the title

quite fitting. A wish come true--a wish that I have probably
made on countless merrythoughts.   And it makes me very
happy. I hope it makes you happy, too. And I hope it makes
you think, "Hmm. If she did it, so can I."   Whatever your
IT might be.

I'm closing my eyes right now and making a wish.

And the wish is saying that,
whatever your IT might be,
I want you to DO IT and HAVE IT.

To Dream Is To Believe

❧

My grandfather died when I was three and a half years old. He was a chocolate salesman and an exceptionally kind, affectionate man who loved children. He wore thin sweaters that buttoned up the front over his "bay window," as my aunt called his big belly, and I remember sitting on his lap in my grandparents' front room. For a long time I had this memory of the day he died:

My mother and sisters and I were standing at the dining room window watching him walk up the hill in front of our house.

I said, "Where's Grandpa going, Mommy?"

And she said, "He's going up to heaven."

We stood there and watched him walk until we couldn't see him anymore.

It must have been a dream, but it was so vivid in my young mind that my brain recorded it as a memory, until I was old enough to realize that of course it could not have been real. Although what, after all, is real? That was as real as

anything else I remember from childhood. And it made me happy to think that he was just walking up the hill to heaven. I was disappointed, later, to have the adult realization that it was just a dream.

I'm writing this on a cool, drizzly, dreamy sort of day, one on which it seems like anything could be counted as real and Any Thing could be counted as a dream, and the line that divides the two is a dotted one that curves, with little spaces that you could squeeze between if you really wanted to. It's the sort of day on which I imagine I could build a treehouse to live in and have polite, well-mannered squirrels to tea. And birds would come and decorate my hair with bits of stuff they'd find way down there in the yard while I dangle my legs from a tree branch, surveying the neighborhood through a spyglass.

On days like this I believe that anything is possible, that I could take a small boat out on the sea and go adventuring. Or that I could finish this book and many others and be someone who writes books in a pretty little villa in Italy or France, and in between times take long walks through the

mists and fog on the Isle of Skye. It's a great day for dreaming up and nurturing the wildest, most marvelous plans imaginable. But then, couldn't any day be great for that, after all? For it's in dreaming that we allow ourselves to know who we are and what we want.

I just wonder and I'll ask, as if you and I were having tea together in my treehouse,

"What are your dreams?"
"What would you dream if you could dream up anything at all?"

Goethe said that anything you dream you can do, you can.

God loves dreamers--you, me, Goethe, all of us.

dream

EXPLORE

COMMIT

He dreamed of elephants every night until, finally, one day he went off on safari to Africa. The elephants there were much smaller than he had imagined, so he went back home and was content to dream.

"DREAM BIG,"
she said.

"For example, I dream of one day building myself a grand treehouse to live in, and having flowers and chocolate brought up every morning. A N Y T H I N G can happen, you know."

One day
she vowed to
become proficient at
croquet and to
spend rainy
Saturdays drinking
cups of tea and
reading British
mystery novels.
"Ah yes," she said.
"A civilized life
at last."

In my bedroom
my poodle snores.
Old man.
A white curve of curly hair
fitted perfectly into his
round bed.
Mine is a box.
Who dreams better?

ONE
~~AFTER~~
~~ANOTHER~~
these wild sweet
mornings arrive
at my house,
declaring that
EVERY
single
THiNG is
POSSiBLE.

One day

I shall live in a treehouse. A large one, of course,
with many windows & balconies
     & a variety of perches where I can sit & read
    or take out a spyglass & see what
        other people (& the birds) are doing.
    And a nice cozy bedroom that is ALL bed &
pillows, with a skylight in the roof for moon-gazing. And
    a hobbit-sized kitchen with just two of everything,
two cups, two plates, two spoons, & so forth.

Oh, yes. One day.

Take your disbelief and toss it out the window.

You don't need it.

I have come to love
the soulful grey
days almost as
much as the bright,
beautiful ones.
It's just that I'm
better able to
settle comfortably
and dream dreams
without the
engaging chatter
of the sun just
outside the
window.

Life With Dogs & Other Living Creatures

~

I have a feral farm poodle with a shaggy hairdo ("No poufs or puffs," I always say) who loves roaming in woods and wild places (with me, of course). He was born in the woods and his heart is in the woods. But in social settings, he is quite well-mannered, and he loves all dogs and all people. Once in a great while, when it gets very cold and his hair has been cut too short, my son puts him in a hideous orange argyle sweater, claiming it is "awesome." And every February he wears a red satin bowtie for my annual MidWinter's Eve Party.

One day I did a piece of art with a long verse about my dog and me. The writing came out all in a rush, as writing sometimes does, and then the collage did, too, with much merriment on my part, as I cut, arranged and pasted the pieces.

In June I took the "White Poodle" collage to a show in

Iowa City and a woman came into my booth and fell right in love with it. She turned back and forth between that piece and another rather grand one called "Hats." I became quite nervous as she turned first to one and then to the other, for I knew, suddenly, that I loved the "White Poodle" too much to sell it. Finally the woman said that she herself had a Scottish terrier at home who might be offended by a collage about a poodle. And so she bought the "Hats" piece. After she left, I breathlessly wrote NFS (Not For Sale) on a sticker and put it on the "White Poodle" and I never took it to a show again. Now I want to share that writing with you.

I always wanted a small, white, furry dog, & now that I have my own white poodle who loves all dogs & all people, & loves me above all others, I imagine that, even as an old woman, I'll have a white poodle, & he'll adore me like this one does, & follow me everywhere I go & lie at my feet, like this one does, under the desk while I'm working, or under the piano, or wherever I might be, & maybe he'll even learn to sit at the table like poodles in Paris do, or maybe we'll go & live in Paris, he & I, and he'll snack on pieces of croissant or baguette & bits of overripe cheeses

from the fromagerie & we'll take our walks in the Jardins du Luxembourg & gaze at the beautiful statues, & maybe after some years, we'll tire of cheese & bread & we'll live in Santa Cruz, California, where my career dream of selling tickets to the roller coaster will finally come true, & every night after the boardwalk is closed down he & I will take a spin up & down & all around the tracks, since we'll be fast friends with the roller coaster operator, who will also have a small dog (a schnauzer), who loves all dogs & all people. And then my white poodle & I will walk home along the beach in the moonlight.

People have said that I could have sold that collage and made another like it. Oh no. It was the joy I had in doing it that meant so much to me, and that is why it must live at my house.

And my poodle might have been offended.
Dogs know things.

"YOU ARE NOT
A **REAL DOG**,"
SHE WOULD OFTEN
REMIND HIM,
"ONLY A FRENCH POODLE."

BUT SHE KISSED THE TOP
OF HIS CURLY LITTLE HEAD
AND GAVE HIM A SMALL
ARTIFICIAL BONE,
WHICH HE BURIED
THOUGHTFULLY

UNDER HER BED PILLOW.

"In Paris," she told her little poodle, "dogs like you a c c o m p a n y their owners to f a s h i o n a b l e restaurants. But NOT in America." And she shooed him from the table.

The birds
in my yard
have been very
encouraging
this spring.
Even when the
weather is awful,
they sing as if it
is lovely.

The young dragonfly,
or nymph, lives underwater for
FIVE years, comes into the sunlight
to fly and mate for just a few weeks,
and then dies. What a simple life,
spent mostly in cool, dark not-
knowing, and the last glorious bit
making love in the
summer sun! We
humans
could never manage it. We WANT
far too much.

She fed the birds
every day
but a fat grey squirrel came along
& ate everything before they got
much. She decided to change her
way of thinking.

"I'm feeding that
grey squirrel &
*I hope to God the birds
don't get to it first.*"
It made her very
happy.

Oh it thunders & rumbles
trees blowing this way & that.
Michael said he wanted
for his wedding day
a sunny morning
& stormy night.
I'll take that too okay God?
And let's see
how about ever
& always a dog (a poodle)
like mine
or better yet this very one
breaking all records
for poodle longevity
staying at his peak
in his prime
until the day he dies
on the day I die
& we both can go
lying on the couch
together
snoring.

THE SUN
CAME OUT AND
THE WHOLE TOWN
BREATHED A SIGH
OF RELIEF★★EVEN
THE DOGS, WHO
TEND TO LOVE
SNOW.

O let me be
a squirrel
a red one
with a fabulous tail.
I will abandon myself to Now
wholly, bodily in my world
of trees earth telephone wires rooftops
making impossible leaps
from branch to tiny unlikely branch
thinking not of whether or not
nor of wish and why or why not
knowing nothing
knowing All
in my wild acrobat's body
tiny Buddha of the backyard.

A cold sunny morning before Christmas
and my mind has turned already to the promise
of a year that's new with plans of unburdening my heart,
conspiring with ritual, whimsy, and symbolism
to do the deed of tossing over all that
impedes the speed of my battered old boat.
And as I write, my dog, with light spirit ever
uncomplicated asks most patiently to be taken
out where he unloosed will run wild and happy
full on, no book, guru, or pithy quote providing
inspiration, his untamed instinct for joy relying on
no one and nothing, requiring only the click
of the leash removed.

IMAGINATION

IS

EXCELLENT

Imagination Is Excellent

One of my favorite books is the real *Peter Pan*, by James M. Barrie. In it, Neverland is a real place children go, and the line between Real and Imaginary is comfortably loose. Mrs. Darling rummages in her children's minds at night (as all mothers do), straightening them out as if they were tiny bureau drawers. She finds things about Neverland and the word "Peter" scattered amongst their many thoughts, and she nervously folds and tucks them far to the back, under less disturbing things. The Lost Boys and Peter and Wendy eat pretend meals and become so caught up in their make-believe that the boys tell on each other for "starting with cheese-cakes," and so forth.

Oh, children have it all over us adults, with their wild and wonderful imaginations, pretend and make-believe, crazy stories, and belief in all manner of marvelous things, like giants, dragons, and monsters. Imagination lives outside the realm of conscious thought. It exists far past the boundaries

of Probable and Likely, lies at the top of children's disorderly minds and way at the back of adults', underneath piles of telephone numbers, tax benefits, depreciation tables, why the world is in such terrible shape, who said what about whom or what, who's to blame for the state of the economy, and why we can't find a decent parking space downtown anymore. We seem to spend a good deal of time arranging our brains so that all the tiresome old thoughts are right on top and our odd little quirky ideas (like, "Maybe I'll wear my duck pants to work today," or "What if I painted poems all over my car?") get wadded up and stuffed into a back corner.

**Albert Einstein himself said,
"Imagination is more important than knowledge."**

You'd think that if Albert Einstein could make such a statement, more of us would pay attention to it. Personally, I do not like facts and figures. I feel a certain dullness settling over my brain when presented with too many facts or an excess of numbers. Graphs and flow charts, in particular,

seem to have a soporific effect on me. I have a terrible time remembering facts ("Was it *genes* or *chromosomes*??"), even when I want to, and I cannot measure and be precise, no matter how important it might be to do so. Naturally, I adore Einstein for his remark, and if he wasn't dead, I would like to kiss the top of his fluffy white head.

Einstein was considered a dullard in elementary school, most likely because his teachers wanted him to give the answers they'd already thought up, whereas his young, spirited brain was whirring away, imagining all sorts of other, much more fascinating things. And people say, Ah, if only we all used as much of our brains as he did! But maybe we just don't use our IMAGINATIONS as much as we ought. What about THAT?

Imagination exercises the brain.

And the *heart*, too.

As a child, I did not like school and even now, I am tempted, when passing a schoolyard, to throw open the gates and call out, "You're free! Go! Go! You're free!!" And watch, smiling, as all the children run gaily off to play their own games, no bell or buzzer telling them when to STOP.

If you pretend
that LIFE is
exciting,
it will be.
That's
just how our

hearts

work.

Whenever he was sick,
she would read
to him from
"Alice in Wonderland"
until he drifted off
to sleep like
the Dormouse.
She always made sure
he didn't go
NOSE FIRST
into his
teacup,
though.

"Grab on!" she cried
& I did
but the roller coaster was
going so fast that I
flew off
&   landed on top of the
ticketseller's booth.
She gave me a
FREE RIDE
next time around.

Today
I don't care for discipline
or doing what I should do.
I want to climb a tree
step into a storybook
have tea with talking creatures
in tophats and pocketwatches.
I want my next trip
to take place on the back of a flying beast
who is also my best friend
and who cries out in a beastly voice,
"Hold on!" in the tight turns.
I want the storybook to have a thick old cover
and faded, gold-flecked pictures
into which I, tiny and flat,
will wander wherever I please
in make believe.
(Just for today.)
I promise to come back
and do my work
tomorrow.

One spring day, they took
tea & cookies out to the
garden for a little party.
All too quickly, the
chocolate dipped ones
began to melt in the sun.

"Oh no!" they cried.

But rather than go
indoors, they decided to just
eat all the chocolate ones
in a hurry.

And that was that.

Occasionally,
her afternoon
tea ran
RIGHT into
cocktail hour,
and there was
just nothing
she could do
about it.

Ooh la la and loo loo lay
it's an Alice in Wonderland sort of day!
Pretend life's exciting grand and swell
the world is our oyster and I can tell
that anything can happen on a rainygreen day
everything's possible let's work not play
make something wondrousgrand and oh so sweet
on this openingup day and follow two feet
to AnywhereAnythingAnywho hey
It's a brand new morning of a great big day.

When she was
young, she rode
bareback in the

CIRCUS.

Now she goes
barefoot
down the road
every morning
to get the paper,
her long grey hair
streaming out
behind her.

The horse stays in the yard.

Love,
Romance
and
ALL

Love, Romance, & All
❻

When my second son was 10 years old, his teacher asked the class to write about love. His competitive spirit moved him to put down as much as he could, as quickly as he could. This is what he came up with.

"The important thing about love is that everyone has some. It makes you happy, it comes from the heart, it is wonderful, it makes marriage, it brings hugges [sic] and kisses, it makes people come together, it makes new life, it makes you feel good, it makes friends, it's sweet, it is joyful, people share with it, it makes people feel warmth, it helps people care for each other, it makes you feel merry, it makes you want to give, it brings happiness to all, everyone wants to be loved, it brings laughter, compliments come from love, love makes friendship grow, it helps people be in groups, it makes people sad when death comes, it brings children to love, it keeps the world together, love makes what they are, it makes strong feelings, it travels from heart to heart and makes more, but the important

thing about love is everyone has some."

I feel blessed that he knew in his bones what love is all about, and that he was able to put it so eloquently at the tender age of ten. As you might imagine, I keep these words (in his delightful ten-year-old handwriting) in my livingroom, just in case anyone needs reminding. Now that my sons are grown and live elsewhere, it's a good reminder for me, too, of all the things that love is and should be.

Love and romance, and falling in love and loving are things I write about again and again, for Valentine's Day and birthdays and so forth, and even though we True Romantics sortof think along those lines most of the time, it also comes with the occupation of making greeting cards. Again and again I have the task of figuring out what I can say about love that's new and fresh. Luckily for me (and for all of us), human beings and our hearts are so remarkable and complex that there is always another charming, bittersweet, or wonderful love story to be told or dreamed up. And so I draw on the many notions about love and romance that have captured my imagination from movies and books, as well as the many real-

life chapters and short stories that I have heard or lived. I am confident that the world will continue to provide one after another.

Each of us has at least one love story to tell, one that we've lived or heard or imagined and lean toward with hope. Each of us has the deep capacity for love and romance, whether we leap the cliff again and again or just once for life, or even if we haven't quite gotten there yet. Always, if we let it, love enlarges us, whether it's love of self, friend, child, or lover, and no matter how it turns out in the end.

And if you haven't quite been there yet, or if you've dug down deep and loved and lost, or if you've tried time and time again and it hasn't been quite right, well, probably things are unfolding at this very moment just as they should.

And one day, oh yes, one day love will happen.
Just you wait and see.

One day you'll find *love*

I KNOW you will,
after all the years & all the false starts,
it will happen, **BOOM!** from out of nowhere
& you'll call me on the telephone or we'll meet
in coffee shops to tell all the wonderful little details,
like for instance, oh, the laughing eyes & gentle touch,
& the sweet, secret names you'll give each other,
the promises given & plans made
& the little gifts offered back & forth.
Oh yes, one day it WILL happen.
Just you wait & see.

she was not italian
but she could speak
english with an
italian accent
& she became
very ~~romantic~~
whenever the tips of his
fingers smelled of garlic

He called her
"sweetie" and
"crumbcake"
and "darling"
and "baby" and
all the things
(& more) that
she ever
wanted to be
called. By
contrast, she
called him
"dumbhead."
A classic case
of opposites
attracting.

One day maybe
we'll live in
Italy in a
little old
ramshackle
house with
vines growing
up over the
windows, a
small wiry dog
running loose,
and masses of
thyme wandering
all over the
yard. Ah,yes,
one day. But
until then,
let's just LOVE
each other.

He called her up every morning to report this or that bit of information, for example, that he had seen a redheaded woodpecker whose head was NOT red, or that the raccoons had gotten into his melons again, or to try out yet another fake accent on her. Or just to say that he loved her, which was what all the other bits of information were really about, anyway.

She called him up every morning to report this or that bit of information, for example, that some extinct forms of dragonflies had wingspans of up to two and a half feet, or that she had seen a wild turkey right in her yard, in the middle of town! Or just to say that she loved him, which was what all the other bits of information were really about, anyway.

Oh,
how the neighbors
talked! First, there was
that little twinkle
in her eye.
Then, of course, there
were the many *hats*.
Opera music was
heard coming from her
house. *&* she was seen
building a
treehouse (of all things!)
in the backyard.
She was
in love.

"I may be getting up in years, but once in a blue moon I get those little romantic feelings. IF you know what I mean," she said with a little wink.

F i n a l l y ,
the day came when they
were to be married.
& even though it
rained, the birds
a n n o u n c e d
the event to the world
as if it were a
beautiful day. Which,
of course, in their
two hearts, it really

W a s .

Oh rumble & crack
you moody firmament
and bring on any & all
romantic notions of
wooden ships at sea
and houses set in trees
me and my true love
abed just so for all the day
no, huddled inside a cave
our green canoe anchored
downside up or even no
in some woodland cabin
where we cannot but stay
eschewing work and company
and I in tousled disarray
of robe and uncombed hair
shall bake some kind of cake
with surprises in while he
middle aged in spectacles
studies a book on home repair
but sneaks from time to time up
and wrapping sturdy arms around
presses one sweet kiss upon my head.

Tomorrow & the next day

& the day after that & the day after that
I want to wake up knowing that
you love me
& I want you to wake up knowing that
I love you.
And that's all.
That's enough.
That's it in a nutshell
the whole nine yards
the whole kit & caboodle
the whole shooting match
the end of the story.

The World of Work

(IN WHICH SOME OF US RUN AWAY

AND ARE FOUND SOMEPLACE ELSE

ENTIRELY)

The World of Work
(In Which Some of Us Run Away & Are Found
Someplace Else Entirely)

6

My business card reads Kay Foley, DILETTANTE. I get a little private laugh each time I hand it out, whether or not the recipient knows what the word means. I have wanted just such a business card for a long, long time, and now that my work is writing, art, and music, I believe I can honestly claim to be a dilettante. My father would be proud.

DILETTANTE: a person with an amateurish or superficial interest in the arts; a lover of the fine arts; a connoisseur. The Italian *dilettare*, lover of the arts, is derived from the Latin word, *delectare*, to delight. Well, isn't this lovely? My job title contains many excellent words that are close to my heart, words such as *lover*, *fine arts*, *connoisseur*, and *delight*! Thus I use the word most contentedly.

Work has been many things to me. As a child I went

door to door selling potholders made out of those colorful stretchy loops. In high school my best friend and I had a dancing school in the church basement. She taught kids to dance and I played the piano. Every Saturday we went downtown on the bus and spent all the money we earned.

As an adult I worked as a typist at a shoe company, a medical book publisher, and an insurance investigation company in San Francisco. I tried selling art and cards in Union Square, too. Back then, I had a clear vision for my life. I would be a writer and artist, working alone and with others on all sorts of wonderful creative projects--books, art, plays, etc. Like most people, I got sidetracked. I married, worked in my then husband's bike shop, worked as a secretary, gave piano lessons, had children, made and sold crafts, and eventually went to college, then graduate school as an older, working, single mother. My goal was to be a counseling psychologist.

It took years and years to get my two degrees. With my Master's, I ran a wellness program at a women's college, then worked as a therapist in a women's drug and alcohol treatment center. I wistfully recalled that 20-year-old vision from time

to time, but most especially and vividly when I read Julia Cameron's marvelous book, *The Artist's Way*.

Her book reminded me of a world I had always wanted to live in. Eventually, I just took a leap! Left my heartbreaking work in the treatment center, started writing and making cards, and teaching piano. Oh, it sounds simple, doesn't it? It was and it wasn't, and I did struggle, and I still do. I keep myself afloat in a variety of ways, and I am lucky in that regard. I'm a good typist, I remind myself. I can always be a secretary if I can't make this work. But I wanted to bring joy back into my life, and I had gifts to use--a vision to follow.

I think we all need to let our gifts speak to us, discover where our joy lies, and follow a path that delights us, at least part, if not most, of the time.

We all have gifts.
Accept yours gracefully--and use them.
❻

I decided that the
world of work is
not conducive to
joy--and so I
became a dreamer
of dreams that
come true. I'm much
h a p p i e r
N   O   W   .

DO THE THING
YOU LOVE MORE THAN
ANYTHING IN LIFE! YOU
MIGHT BECOME A BIT
UNPREDICTABLE (SOMETIMES
CRANKY), BUT YOU WILL BE
HAPPIER THAN YOU EVER
IMAGINED
POSSIBLE.

He wanted to run away to the
circus
but he felt he was
(alas!) too old

& the circus was

(sigh!) too far from home.
He went to the movies,
instead & it turned out
that he was
pretty happy
about it
after all.

Upon entering middle age, she developed a *fondness* for umbrellas & galoshes & noisy spring thunderstorms. And now her friends find her wandering *contentedly* through puddles when she REALLY SHOULD be working.

"AT LAST," HE SIGHED, "I'M FINISHED WITH SCHOOL AND I CAN WORK, ONCE AND FOR ALL, IN ONE OF THOSE MINT GREEN OFFICES." WELL, ALL I CAN SAY IS, EVERYONE'S GOT TO HAVE A DREAM.

She daydreamed about being a hot air balloon pilot or a hatmaker. One day she up & walked out of the factory and took off down the road. I never saw her again, but one time she sent me a photograph of herself riding on the back of an elephant. My, but she l o o k e d h a p p y !

His fondest wish was
that one day, out of the
blue, he would be
offered a job
taste-testing French
olives & wines.
He would also be
REQUIRED to travel to
the south of France
SEVERAL TIMES A YEAR.

ONE DAY
SHE WOULD BE A CAT
BURGLAR, SHE VOWED,
CREEPING IN AND OUT OF
FANCY HOUSES--NOT SO
MUCH FOR THE DIAMONDS
(ALTHOUGH ACCESSORIES ARE
ALL IMPORTANT)
BUT JUST SO SHE COULD
WEAR THE

OUTFIT.

My father's father
wanted him to work
for the telephone
company, but my
father followed his HEART
and went to college,
instead. We kids
learned a great lesson
from that.

IT IS NOT
WHAT
YOU'VE
DONE
THAT
MATTERS,
BUT THE
ACT OF
DOING
IT.

Get quiet & listen to
what is
most
important
to you & run towards it
with an open
HEART.

pondering the BIGGER questions of life

Pondering the Bigger Questions of Life

ξ

"How much air is between my face and my hand if I hold it right here?"

My oldest son was four years old when he asked me that rather difficult question. Yikes! I could not even imagine an answer. And that's the great thing about our brains. When we are most alive, we ask the questions that have no answers. And sometimes we spend *lots* of time with them. And if we're *really* thinking, feeling, imagining, and *open*, we come to accept that NOT KNOWING might be the truest wisdom.

And sometimes not knowing is just more enjoyable. It leaves more room for the imagination and gives us that child-like wonderment and awe. When I was a child, I spent a windy afternoon trying to figure out whether the wind blew the trees or the trees made the breeze blow my hair. (I know, this seems a bit ridiculous, but I wasn't sure.) That process of

working on the question was much more intriguing to my young mind than the rather dull fact that tree branches are still until the wind blows them (aren't they?). I wondered, too, why boys' hair did not grow any longer than a crewcut (this was in the '50s). The questions themselves were far more interesting than the answers, for I remember vividly the process of watching, seeing, thinking, and theorizing, but I have no memory of finding out the dumb old answers.

Gertrude Stein said that anything you can know is not interesting.

Of course, some answers, when they come, bring that rush of centering relief, that lovely inner calm, that feeling of a smooth piece sliding easily into its right place, that "Ahhh" feeling that comes only after *wanting* to know and working on the problem.

Certainly there are those bigger questions that all thinking persons ask at some point during their lives. Is there a God? Is there a purpose to life? Is there an absolute right

and wrong? What is the soul (if it exists)? Are we reincarnated? Or is there nothing at all, after death? Are there such things as innate goodness, a collective unconscious, the human condition? What is knowledge? What is imagination?

Then there are our own odd little questions. Are snakes really evil? Do dogs go to heaven? Why do people tend to ridicule people who live in the state just south of them? Why do all dogs everywhere bark at the mailman? Etc.

These are questions for which we do not have answers, or at least, no factual answers. We can have wonderful, thoughtful, and insightful theories but we can't KNOW.

**And the not-knowing is, to me, a beautiful thing.
A treasure. A sign of wisdom.**

That's the real beauty.

ろ

I resolved to
surround myself
with
EXPLORERS
who are not afraid
to wander the back
roads of their
minds.
Luckily for me,
I enjoy

small, intimate parties.

She ate many
chocolate truffles
while pondering the
BIGGER
questions of life.
It didn't help her
thought process but
it did make the
whole enterprise
more enjoyable.

STRUGGLE WITH YOUR QUESTIONS AND, AS RILKE SAID, LOVE THEM.

Develop the patience of a rock, I tell myself. Accept that time and life do what they will, trusting that they make us who we are, in the end.

I believe it is good to
S   T   U   D   Y
the influence of somebody
upon something (as Virginia
Woolf would say) ,but
ENOUGH'S
ENOUGH!

She said
her brain
had too
many
things in
it and
she was
trying to
get rid
of the
stuff she
didn't
need
anymore.
Some of
it just
wouldn't
budge,
though.

It is our belief in GOODNESS that lifts us up and over and beyond all that's ugly and tragic in the world. To keep that belief alive, that's the trick. That's the hard (but entirely possible) part.

Maybe when we
die, our Real Selves
shake off the
confines of our
skin & bones
& even those who
never danced or
turned cartwheels
on Earth will
pirouette & spin
lightly, gaily,
gorgeously
through the
cosmos.

Magic,
the
Moon
& the
Insanely
Beautiful
World
in
Which
We
Live

Magic, the Moon & the Insanely Beautiful World in Which We Live

﹖

There are places on this earth that I love beyond others. That goes without saying. There is a woods I go to, here in my hometown of Columbia MO, officially called a "wild area" (I love that), a little pocket of wildness surrounded by peoples' houses and cattle farms and such. Sometimes it seems to me that there is *everything* in those woods. There are maple groves that, in October, are so brilliantly, marvelously, yellowly yellow that even on a rainy day it seems as if the sun is bursting through. "Uh-oh," I say to my feral poodle, as we enter yet another magnificent grove of maples, "More beauty." It's the kind of place that makes my heart ache with tenderness.

There are bluffs overlooking a meandering creek, beautiful rocky bluffs with many lookout spots where one can

sit and gaze or ponder or write a line or two or eat a sandwich or just do nothing. And there's the creek itself, with its pleasant, affable chatter about nothing in particular, idly going about its business, never noticing that it is the heart of the whole place. It is the thing that makes bluffs bluffs. It is the Danny Kaye of the Danny Kaye Show.

There are big mossy rocks there, and tiny and large caves at once mysterious and seductive, and little gullies full of blue-ball cedar trees and winding paths. There's a fallen log to play on, a pileated woodpecker that I hear but never see, the silent, distinguished skeleton of a once perfect and now perfectly bare cedar tree, and even the stone chimney of an old cabin where some lucky person once lived a hard life in the wildnerness. All of that in those woods.

Well, that is just one little spot on this earth of ours, and it's a humble one at that, when you consider places like the Grand Canyon, the Rocky Mountains, the Everglades, etc. But natural beauty is not a contest and all places, great and small, are magical to those who look.

I do my writing in a tiny, draughty room in the back of

my house. The windows don't seal well, and the floor is mighty cold in winter. In summer, the room heats up in a hurry, and wasps manage to find their way in to bother. It's tiny and cramped and I am always moving piles of things from here to there, to do my work.

But I have windows all the way across three sides of the room, a mimosa tree whose branches spread out along two sides, and a birdfeeder that brings me a happy parade of chickadees, titmice, finches, cardinals, and squirrels. I can watch the sun and moon come up through the east windows and the twilight settle at day's end at the west. As cold, hot, and inconvenient as it is, it is open to a world I want to soak up, any time of year. A lovely spot in which to collect my thoughts.

The beauty out there can be almost too much to bear.

Must be magic.
Ş

Sometimes

she became
overwhelmed
by the beauty
of life--and then
she could do nothing
but shut her eyes
and pretend she was
already an
angel.

Make my
bed with
daffodils,
not roses--
for
daffodils
are so
hopeful.

Our town grew weary of the
weather reports last February and
petitioned the City Council
to ban them.
Now we have
SPRING
all year long.

"BRING YOUR HAT,
FOR IT IS SURE TO BE WINDY
OUT ON THE OCEAN," HE SAID.
BUT I ADORE
THE SMELL OF THE
SEA AIR IN MY HAIR
AND PRETENDED TO HAVE
FORGOT MINE.

IT WAS LOVELY.

The dragonfly, with its gossamer wings and slender body, is unafraid to light upon the toe of a human or even to MAKE LOVE while perched delicately upon self-same toe. Oh, what we miss with our human caution!

VENUS

IS COURTING THE
MOON TONIGHT.
SHE'S PUT ON HER
PRETTIEST *party dress*,
SLIPPED OUT OF HER
dainty shoes, *&* LET
THAT LONG, SILVER
HAIR SPILL DOWN HER
BACK. *&* THE *sparks*
FROM THEIR ROMANCE
(WE CALL THEM STARS)
HAVE *lit up* OUR
LITTLE WORLD.

91

On Christmas Eve a long time ago, my sister swore she heard reindeer hooves on the roof. I believed her then & I believe her still today. We can all use a little extra magic in our lives I always say.

Tell me
about the moon,
for I don't get it. No, DON'T.
Let me be surprised.
Let me look and look and look and
not find and then suddenly spot it,
right in my eye, in the wrong part of
the sky. And I'll laugh right out
loud. Let me wonder where it goes
and why it is there in daylight
sometimes but not always. Don't
spoil my fun with facts and charts.
I want to be
                    enchanted.

Mimosa leaf pattern on the glass
tells that beauty is everywhere
and all things are possible.

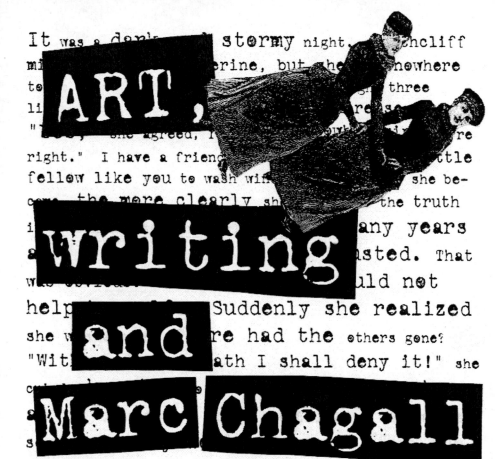

ART, writing and Marc Chagall

Art, Writing, & Marc Chagall

⌐•

I have been to France twice. Twice to Paris and once to Nice. And while in Nice I saw the incredible cut-outs of Henri Matisse--the Jazz series--as well as some other beautiful cut-outs. I had my photograph taken in front of a magnificent piece that took up one huge wall. And once I went to the Tower at the National Gallery in Washington, D.C., which is filled completely with five or six huge Matisse cut-outs. They are breathtaking! Matisse made them when he was ill and too weak to paint. And yet they are full of light, movement, joy, and life.

I went once with my sisters to see a wonderful exhibit of Marc Chagall's paintings at the San Francisco Museum of Modern art. These works of art bring me so much joy. So much that my body feels full and light, like a long, thin me-shaped balloon that could easily float up into a blue blue sky, just like Chagall's people do, like the beautiful painted shapes

hovering in their places in Matisse's wonderful cut-outs.

Picasso once said, "Art washes from the soul the dust of ordinary life."

Certain works of art do that for me and so I love them. Chagall makes love visible right there on the canvas. A boy rides a giant rooster with his arms around its neck, a bride and groom float above a little town, a woman in a white dress is held tenderly by a goat dressed in a man's suit. He takes us two steps away from ordinary life. Yes, he says, anything is possible.

Writing, too, has that wonderful quality. What is writing but letters strung together--black marks on a white page? Yet those marks can charm, excite and mystify, give meaning where we had seen none, move us to tears, inspire us to think and act, or make us laugh right out loud. Regardless of meaning, the shapes of letters, of certain words, and the juxtaposition of certain letters can be quite beautiful.

It is true, too, that writing words down on a page,

whether anyone else sees our writing or not, can lift us out of slumps and take us places we'd like to go, places we sometimes only imagine and have no real experience of. Words written down in the form of intentions and promises to ourselves or others can move us to act, create, and do. Words have the power to liberate us from mental prisons, throw open the French doors on the balconies of our closed up brains, and let light pour in.

They may be just marks on a page, marks we were taught to make at a very young age and ones we now just approximate in our own style or even make with machines, but they are full of meaning and power. My words, your words, Virginia Woolf's words, our children's words--all immensely powerful. Think, for example, of the word YES. Yes, you can paint. Yes, you can write. Yes, you can play the piano.

We are all writers. We are all artists.
We create worlds.

ART
IS
EVERYWHERE.
BUT YOU
HAVE TO
SEE IT.

There's
MAGIC
in my pen,
wonderful
MAGIC.

Each morning before dawn
she brought a cup of tea to
bed & wrote down her many
thoughts on sheets of paper.
"I'll be a writer one day," she
told her little poodle," & we'll
travel ALL OVER the world
& meet the people who buy
my books!" He kept his nose
buried within the curl of his
body, but she could tell that
he believed in her, nonetheless.

Writing makes all things possible.

Take your
inspiration
~~from~~ the
everyday--
children,
birds,
the moon,
a ~~puff of~~
cloud.

"One day," he said,
"I will travel (at last!) to
Paris, where poodles
frequent restaurants
& patisseries appear
on every street corner.
And THEN I'll write
my novel!"

It was those floating
       horses *&* lovers in
Marc Chagall's brilliant blue
paintings that *lit up*
       her imagination,
       like the sun *(sparkling)* on
the ocean right up
                into her eye.
       And always always those
       paintings were what she
          imagined *falling in love*
             would be like.

She was a FANCIFUL
GIRL (all those old movies)
and she let grapevines
grow all along the
clotheslines. Beauty, she
said, was more important
to her than function. By
mid-summer, little
bunches of grapes hung
there like tiny clothes.
It made her HAPPY.

Starting fresh
on a page of white
I can make anything be
for I am the writer
the storyteller
the one who says
this is so and that is so
and thus and such.
And so I can make up a life
that is and isn't
was and wasn't
might have been
and never will be
except on this white page
and inside of me.

Notice
EVERYTHING

Living
LIFE
Rightly

Living Life Rightly
≈

     I have become convinced that the real key to living life wholly, fully, and rightly is openness. Stephen Levine writes in his book, *Who Dies?* about a Hasidic teaching that says we must be ready for whatever life has to offer, and more specifically for a particular event or moment for which each of us was born. The teaching says that what we must do is be ready always, aware always, open to every moment. We must remain in a state of openness, in a state of *not knowing*. We must cultivate an openness to not knowing.

     I love this idea. At middle age, I have begun to feel that not knowing is a sign of wisdom, that admitting that I don't know all, or even most, of the answers is a kind of open door that I don't want to close. When we remain open to the mysteries of life, rather than striving for mastery over it, we experience a richness and wisdom that is otherwise lost to us. When we allow ourselves to remain open and receptive, we are

still and active at once. We have not *become* who we are; we continue to grow, change and develop. We are not things; we are beings.

The word *being* is both a noun and a verb. We can attach the word *being* to other words to give them verbness. He is *being* kind. She is *being* honest. I work at *being* open. We can *be* whatever we want to be. *Being* renders all things possible. Being open to newness and change, to allowing life, love and complexity in our lives, to knowing that our lives are unfolding as they should, however difficult the circumstances might be--these, I think, are key to discovering deeper meaning and happiness.

Of course, it is easy for me to SAY these things. It's much more difficult to actually live by them.

Lately, I have been visited by metaphors of doors. Over and over again, these door analogies appear, and it seems clear that I must pay attention. This first one had a great impact on me, even though it is just a simple little story, and not

particularly profound. A woman tries to open her hotel door and finds that her key does not work. Frustrated, she twists and turns the handle, pulling and shaking the door. Finally, she looks up at the room number and realizes she is trying to open the wrong door. Aha! Here's where I have a real aha moment. *Trying to open the wrong door.* How often have I tried to pry open a closed door only to finally walk away exhausted, frustrated, and unhappy? I have a key, yes, but it might be meant for a door that leads to a much more marvelous place. We all need to be awake, aware and open enough to see the doors to which we have keys, and to have the courage to open them.

Another simple truth, from the writing of Parker Palmer--sometimes we stand gazing longingly at a closed door so long that we don't see the rest of the world. If we'd turn around we'd see that every other last thing is there behind us.

Turn around and look.
Doors are everywhere. Open them.

LAUGH HARD

Dance with
abandon

Sing out loud

Love fiercely

"Sometimes," he said,
"it's worth taking a risk
just for the practice."
So I bought a *new*
kind of tea &

I was very glad
it was
only for
practice.

Imagine yourself filled with JOY. Now keep that thought & it will COME TRUE.

*Let us
make a
ritual of
thanking
each day
for
itself.*

ONCE OR TWICE

IN OUR LIVES, WE
ARE GIVEN THE
CHANCE TO FIND
OUT JUST HOW MUCH
INNER STRENGTH
WE POSSESS.
USUALLY WE FIND
WE HAVE FAR MORE
THAN WE EVER

IMAGINED.

Whenever possible choose ADVENTURE.

ONE DAY
I realized that
true grace and even joy
lay in the ability to
accept what is.
At that moment
I went out the door
and reveled in the
steel grey sky
and bare trees,
knowing that they
are an essential
part of life.

LEARN
THE
FINE
ART
OF
waiting.
IT WILL
COME
IN
HANDY.

SOMETIMES
we just make wrong
choices, and what's
great about being
human is that we can
learn and try to do it
DIFFERENTLY
next time.

OR THE TIME AFTER THAT.

BE
PATIENT.
Sometimes
you have to
learn the same
thing over &
over again.

Keys to a Happy Life

Work hard. **Be compassionate.** plant flowers. Avoid anger, worry, & regret. **BE GRATEFUL FOR WHAT YOU HAVE.** Listen to others. **DANCE AND SING.** Never refuse dessert. PLAY. Cultivate openness. SPEND TIME WITH CHILDREN. **Enjoy the** O U T D O O R S. Spend time alone.

About the Author

When I was a child, I dreamed that my head was a railway station, filled with conductors, ticketsellers, and people coming and going to faraway places, with trains rolling in and chugging out. My head is even more full now, much like an old woman's closet, cluttered with boxes, pots, and jars holding all the colors, shapes, and words that make up my work. Spilling out onto the floor (and into my work) are my love of my three sons, the great old romantic movies of the '30s and '40s, my accumulated hopes, dreams, and beliefs, my love of the natural world and its changing seasons, the assortment of charming children and adults I encounter every day, my St. Louis upbringing in a big Irish/German family, and oh yes, that place in my brain where I swear I can FEEL color and light.

I live in a house that needs work (help!) in Columbia MO with my poodle &, when they are in town, my incredible sons.